©2020 Evin Bail O'Keeffe

The author's intellectual property rights have been asserted. All rights reserved. No part of this publication may be reproduced, stored in a retrieval system, or transmitted in any form or by any means, electronic, mechanical, photocopying, or otherwise, without prior expressed written permission of the copyright holder.

Designer, Publisher, Book Designer, Project Manager
Evin Bail O'Keeffe

Technical Editor
Michael Harrigan

Photography
Niall Twamley (daylight photography) and
Evin Bail O'Keeffe (black light photography)

Stylist
Martina Leahy

Copy Editor
William G. Bail

Knitting Technicians
Breda Bonfield, Clare Hamill, Marseille Marra Bunk, Frankie Lodge, Liz DeVoss, Rebekka K. Steg, Tríona Wallace

Models
Georsan Caruth and Evin Bail O'Keeffe

Photographed on location in Cork City, Ireland.

anchorandbee.com
Published in 2020 by Anchor and Bee,
Cork City, County Cork, Republic of Ireland

A CIP catalogue record for this book is available from the British Library.
ISBN 978-1-910567-06-7 (paperback)
ISBN 978-1-910567-07-4 (ebook)

Designs by Evin Bail O'Keeffe

Photography by Niall Twamley

Technical Editing by Michael Harrigan

Published by Anchor and Bee
Cork, Ireland

Contents

Introduction & Acknowledgements   1
Hand Dyers & Knitting Glossary   2-3

Aerglo Wrap
page 5

Altair Cowl
page 9

Betelgeuse Shawl
page 11

Under Ultraviolet Light

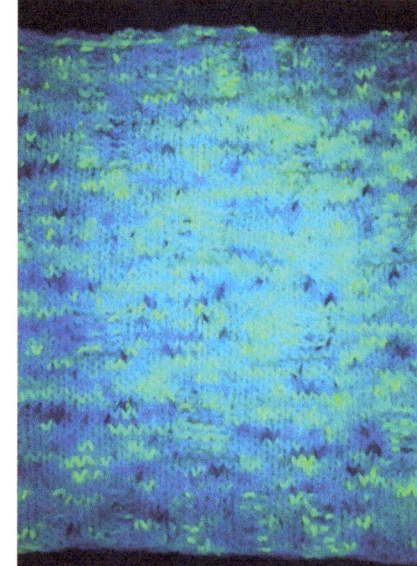

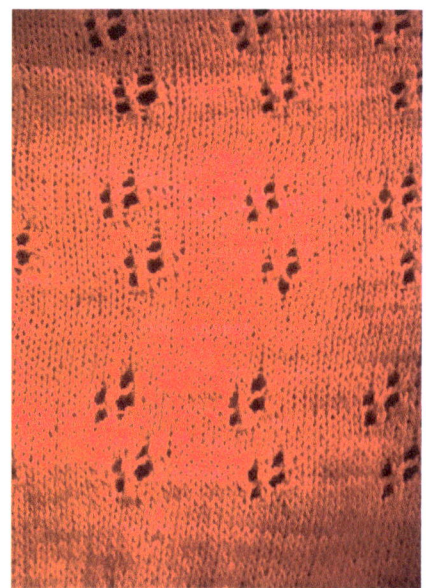

Cassiopeia Mini Skein Shawl
page 15

Elara Shawl
page 19

Firefly Hour Mitts
page 23

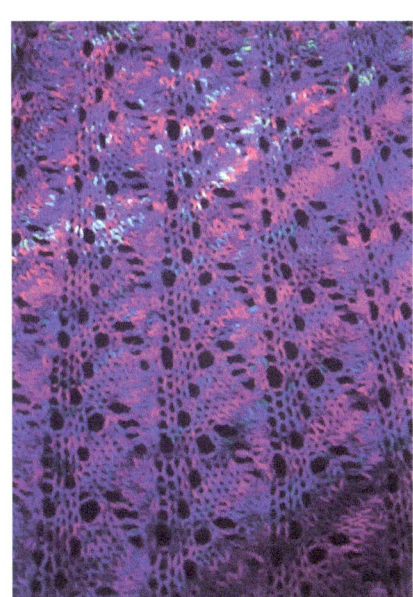

Under Ultraviolet Light

Midnight Waffles Cowl
page 27

Phare Hat
page 29

Porch Light Wrap
page 33

Under Ultraviolet Light

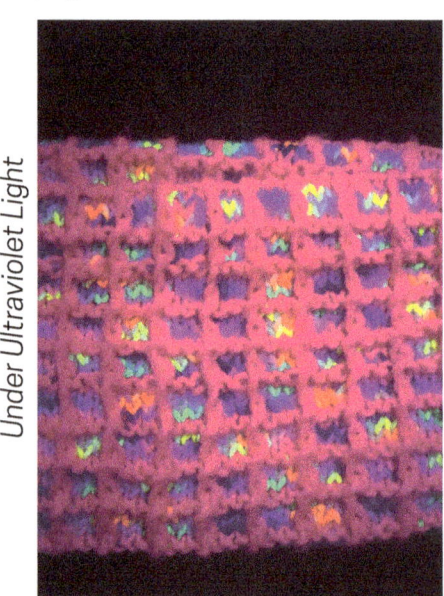

| Rigel Cowl | Rigel Mitts | Wreath Nebula Mitts |
| page 35 | page 39 | page 41 |

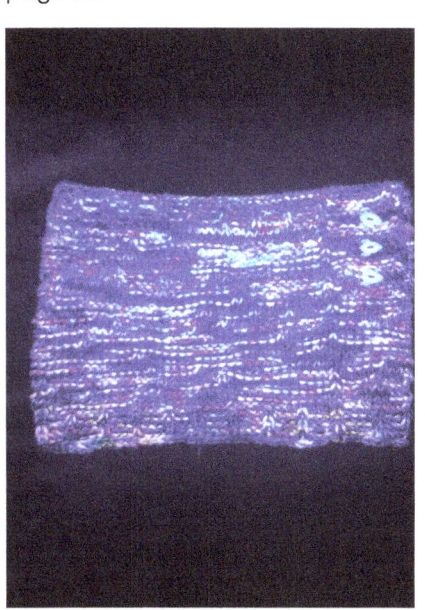
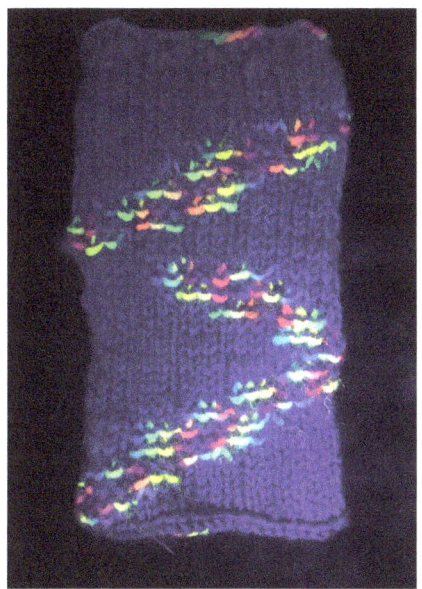
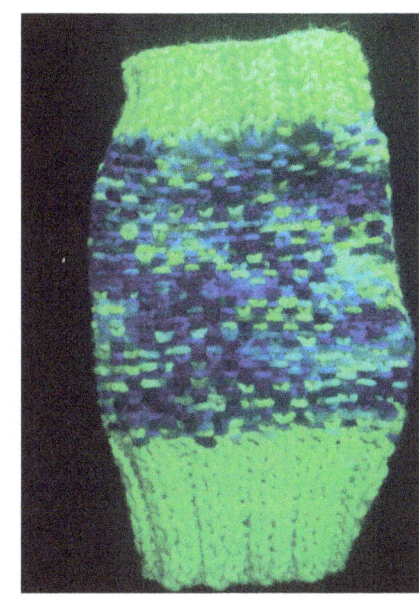

Under Ultraviolet Light

This book includes 12 knitting patterns written to showcase the UV-reactive yarns I've chosen to work with. Half of the projects are inspired by enjoying the night's sky here on Earth, such as star-gazing from a porch swing, while the other patterns pay homage to astronomy.

The idea for this book grew from hearing from a friend about music festivals with ambient black light. Then I wondered if any yarn would glow under black light – and some do! My goal was to create a design that, when knit with this yarn, appears with rich textures as you'd expect, but when the light spectrum changes, the appearance of the design changes as well. Imagine the secret style unveiled when ultraviolet lights go on at the nightclub, rave, or music festival.

I enjoyed the added challenge of designing for yarns that might be speckled, very bright or busy, or even neon. These are often colors which overpower subtle designs or textures. For this reason, the patterns I created are relatively simple but practical, comfortable, and workable for a wide variety of colorways.

This project was a slow, determined, and well planned one… that took three years from idea to book release. The research started when my younger son was six months old and my older son was five years old. The latter helped me test reactivity under black light and sort through my stash to look for dyers I could reach out to. One challenge, of course, is that you cannot tell if a yarn will be UV-reactive from a photo online, unless a black light photo is posted. Sometimes, hand dyers may not even know their yarn is reactive. It's so fun that the yarn has a secret! The collection solidified when I launched my Kickstarter campaign and 57 backers joined me for the final stretch of this project. There were unforeseen obstacles, but nothing insurmountable. Each one was solved as it was faced and though it meant delays, it was a great lesson in perseverance. This book would not be completed today without the enthusiasm and support of my appreciated backers as well as my family and friends. I am especially grateful for the friends who were involved in this project. Thank you for not being embarrassed when I take out my little black light flashlight in local yarn stores!

Aside from learning about how it takes more than a three-year book project to thwart my determination, I also learned a lot as a designer because these designs needed to bring out the reactivity in black light, but for most of their existence they'd be in daylight when they needed to be equally beautiful. One part I enjoyed most was choosing yarns from different dyers to go together.

Throughout the book work, I kept up with my award-winning blog, EvinOK.com – and even won another two awards for its content. The blog is my place to share posts about my craft, food, travel, and life adventures and creations. Please enjoy the additional content available on there, including more knitting patterns and some delectable recipes! You can also see glimpses of these and my everyday life on Instagram, where my username is @freckledpast. If you share your creation on Instagram, use the hashtag #uvknits and tag me so I can admire and reshare it.

I hope you enjoy this book. Thank you for supporting my work by purchasing this collection.

XOXO
Evin Bail O'Keeffe

Yarn Dyers & Buttons

For this book, I chose independent hand dyers who sell their wool yarn online and ship internationally. Here is information on every dyer in this book, plus where I sourced the rocket ship buttons.

Dyer	Website	Instagram
Bear In Sheep's Clothing	bearinsheepsclothing.com	@bearinsheepsclothing
Easy Knits	easyknits.co.uk	@easyknitter
Eve Chambers Textiles	etsy.com/ie/shop/EveChambersTextiles	@evechamberstextiles
Fibre Art Studio	etsy.com/shop/fibreartstudio	@yoriko.oki
GamerCrafting	gamercrafting.com	@gamercrafting
Green Elephant Yarn	greenelephantyarn.com	@greenelephantyarn
La Bien Aimee	labienaimee.com	@labienaimee
Mad Scientist Yarns	madscientistyarns.com	@madscientistyarns
Martin's Lab	martinslab.com	@martinslab
Mothy and the Squid	mothyandthesquid.com	@mothy.and.the.squid
My Mama Knits	mymamaknits.com	@sunshine_stewart
Olann Grá	etsy.com/shop/OlannGra	@olanngra
Qing Fibre	qingfibre.com	@qingfibre
Textile Garden (buttons)	textilegarden.com	@textilegarden
The Wool Kitchen	thewoolkitchen.com	@thewoolkitchen
Uschitita	uschitita.com	@uschitita

Knitting Glossary

Here are terms and abbreviations used in the patterns of this book.

Block - After a knitted garment or item is complete, sometimes the stitches may be uneven or edges may roll. To train the stitches to lay flat or take on a shape, such as a tea cosy, use steam or moisture followed by drying time in a set position. This should not be done on ribbing or other stitches requiring a retention of stretch. Lace knitting is especially transformed when blocked because it goes from compressed and wrinkled to smooth and spread out.

Chart - A visual representation of the stitches in a pattern

Errata - Corrections to any errors in a pattern. If errata exist for this book, they will be posted on the publisher's website at http://anchorandbee.com

Gauge - Number of stitches and rows in a 4-by-4-inch section of knitted material is needed to create the project in the desired size and stitch density.

In the round - This denotes a pattern worked on double-pointed or circular knitting needles. When joining stitches to start knitting in the round, it is important to not twist. One approach to limiting chances of a twist is to cast on an additional stitch which is then shifted to be knitted with the first stitch, thereby joining in the round. If you still find you have a small gap or break in your knitting where you joined in the round, you may use the remaining cast on tail to seam that section together.

K2tog - Knit 2 stitches together at this part of the pattern. This is used as a manner of decreasing stitches, to balance added stitches for a consistent stitch count, or for a design feature.

Kfb - Knit in the front and back of the stitch to increase one stitch.

Kw - Knitwise. The right needle slipping into a stitch on the left needle from left to right, as if to knit the stitch.

Pw - Purlwise. The right needle slipping into a stitch on the left needle in a straight opposing direction (from right to left), as if to purl the stitch.

PM - Place stitch marker.

SM - Slip stitch marker.

RS - Right side. The outside of the fabric or item. What will show to the world when you wear/use it.

WS - Wrong side. The inside of the fabrc or item. What will not show when you wear/use it.

WYIB - With yarn in back

WYIF - With yarn in front

YO - Yarn over. Simply wrap the working yarn around the right needle to create a new stitch.

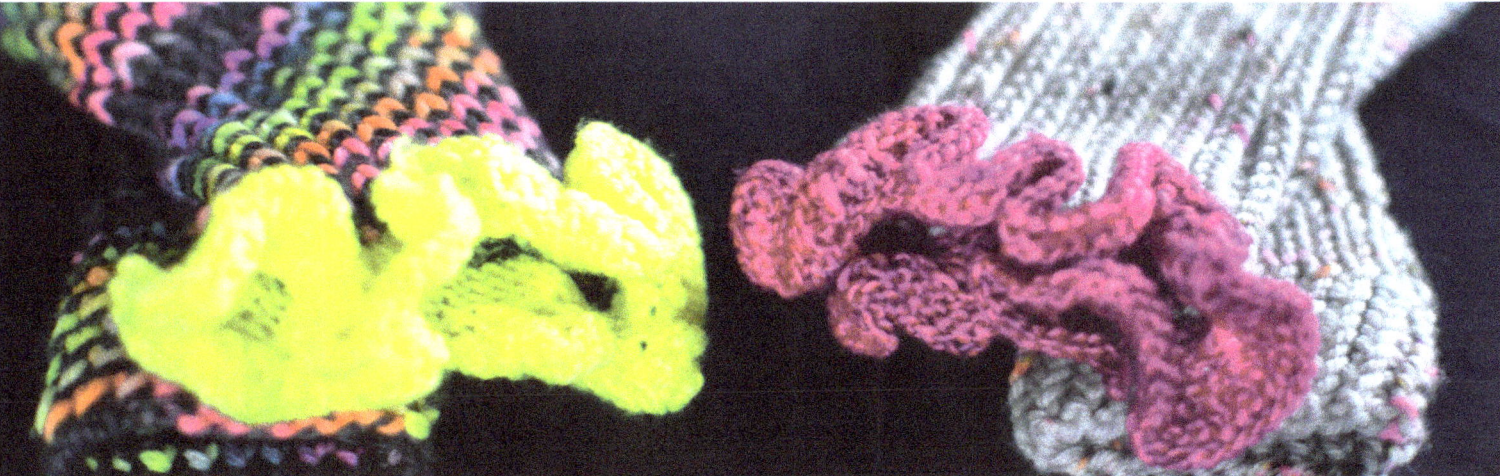

Aerglo Wrap

This shawl can be made in two sizes, both of which are knit using three full skeins and three mini skeins. Each is knit with a background created by the two darker neutral skeins, so the UV-reactive yarn colors pop all the more -- like a pink sunset against a dark creeping ceiling of stars. The construction is very straightforward and much like a triangle shawl, but the result offers extra fabric at the top of the shawl, making it drape nicely for extra neck warmth. The spine of the shawl is a mock cable, in keeping with the shawl's overall appreciation of the slipped stitch.

Weight of Yarn: 1 Super Fine
Skill Level: Intermediate

Sizes: Small and Medium

Finished Measurements:
Small: Height: 55cm. Width: 128cm
Medium: Height: 87cm. Width: 155cm

Materials:
Olann Grá SPORT (328yds/300m, 100g, 100% Superwash Merino): 1 skein Navy (Yarn A)
Mothy and the Squid 4-PLY SOCK (459yds/420m, 100g, 75% Merino Wool, 25% Nylon): 1 skein That's Enough Crazy Pink/Yellow (Yarn B)
Easy Knits TINSEL SOCK (410yds/375m, 100g, 90% Superwash Merino, 10% Lurex): 1 skein Venom (Yarn C)
Mothy and the Squid 4-PLY SOCK MINI SKEINS (91yds/84m, 20g, 75% Merino Wool, 25% Nylon): 1 mini skein Orange/Purple Speckle (Yarn D)
Mothy and the Squid 4-PLY SOCK MINI SKEINS (91yds/84m, 20g, 75% Merino Wool, 25% Nylon): 1 mini skein Purple/Magenta (Yarn E)
Mothy and the Squid 4-PLY SOCK MINI SKEINS (91yds/84m, 20g, 75% Merino Wool, 25% Nylon): 1 mini skein Orange Speckle (Yarn F)
Size US6 (4mm) 24" (60cm) circular needles or size needed to obtain gauge
Stitch marker
Tapestry needle

Gauge: 16 sts and 32 rows = 4 in/10cm.

CO 9 sts, using Yarn A.
Row 1 (RS): K1, yo, *k1, sl1pw (yarn at back), yo, pass k st over sl1 and yo; rep from * to marker, yo, PM, k3, PM, yo, *k1, sl1pw (yarn at back), yo, pass k st over sl1 and yo; rep from * to last st, yo, k1.
Row 2 (WS) and all even-numbered rows: Purl.
Row 3: K1, yo, *k1, sl1pw (yarn at back), yo, pass k st over sl1 and yo; rep from * to marker, yo, SM, k3, SM, yo, *k1, sl1pw (yarn at back), yo, pass k st over sl1 and yo; rep from * to last st, yo, k1.
Row 5: K1, yo, *k1, sl1pw (yarn at back), yo, pass k st over sl1 and yo; rep from * to marker, yo, SM, sl1, k2, psso the two sts, SM, yo, *k1, sl1pw (yarn at back), yo, pass k st over sl1 and yo; rep from * to last st, yo, k1.
Row 7: K1, yo, *k1, sl1pw (yarn at back), yo, pass k st over sl1 and yo; rep from * to marker, yo, SM, k1, yo, k1, SM, yo, *k1, sl1pw (yarn at back), yo, pass k st over sl1 and yo; rep from * to last st, yo, k1.

Row 8: Purl.
Repeat these eight rows to complete shawl.
Bind off loosely.
Block and weave in ends.

Designer Note:
The yarns are knit in sequence as indicated below, but if you prefer striping have fun with it!

For size Small: Switch between yarns every six inches: Navy (Yarn A) (about 18g or 54m), then That's Enough Crazy (Yarn B) (about 36g or 151m), and then Venom (Yarn C) (about 66g or 247m).

For size Medium (using rest of yarn after knitting size Small): Knit with Venom (Yarn C) (about 27g or 101m), then Orange/Purple Speckle 20g mini skein (Yarn D), then Purple/Magenta 20g mini skein (Yarn E), then Orange Speckle 20g mini skein (Yarn F), then Venom (Yarn C) (about 7g or 26m), then That's Enough Crazy (Yarn B) (about 64g or 268m), and then Navy (Yarn A) (about 82g or 246m).

Row 8: Purl.
Repeat these eight rows to complete shawl.
Bind off loosely.
Block and weave in ends.

Designer Note:
The yarns are knit in sequence as indicated below, but if you prefer striping have fun with it!

For size Small: Switch between yarns every six inches: Navy (Yarn A) (about 18g or 54m), then That's Enough Crazy (Yarn B) (about 36g or 151m), and then Venom (Yarn C) (about 66g or 247m).

For size Medium (using rest of yarn after knitting size Small): Knit with Venom (Yarn C) (about 27g or 101m), then Orange/Purple Speckle 20g mini skein (Yarn D), then Purple/Magenta 20g mini skein (Yarn E), then Orange Speckle 20g mini skein (Yarn F), then Venom (Yarn C) (about 7g or 26m), then That's Enough Crazy (Yarn B) (about 64g or 268m), and then Navy (Yarn A) (about 82g or 246m).

Aerglo Wrap

This shawl can be made in two sizes, both of which are knit using three full skeins and three mini skeins. Each is knit with a background created by the two darker neutral skeins, so the UV-reactive yarn colors pop all the more -- like a pink sunset against a dark creeping ceiling of stars. The construction is very straightforward and much like a triangle shawl, but the result offers extra fabric at the top of the shawl, making it drape nicely for extra neck warmth. The spine of the shawl is a mock cable, in keeping with the shawl's overall appreciation of the slipped stitch.

Weight of Yarn: 1 Super Fine
Skill Level: Intermediate

Sizes: Small and Medium

Finished Measurements:
Small: Height: 55cm. Width: 128cm
Medium: Height: 87cm. Width: 155cm

Materials:
Olann Grá SPORT (328yds/300m, 100g, 100% Superwash Merino): 1 skein Navy (Yarn A)
Mothy and the Squid 4-PLY SOCK (459yds/420m, 100g, 75% Merino Wool, 25% Nylon): 1 skein That's Enough Crazy Pink/Yellow (Yarn B)
Easy Knits TINSEL SOCK (410yds/375m, 100g, 90% Superwash Merino, 10% Lurex): 1 skein Venom (Yarn C)
Mothy and the Squid 4-PLY SOCK MINI SKEINS (91yds/84m, 20g, 75% Merino Wool, 25% Nylon): 1 mini skein Orange/Purple Speckle (Yarn D)
Mothy and the Squid 4-PLY SOCK MINI SKEINS (91yds/84m, 20g, 75% Merino Wool, 25% Nylon): 1 mini skein Purple/Magenta (Yarn E)
Mothy and the Squid 4-PLY SOCK MINI SKEINS (91yds/84m, 20g, 75% Merino Wool, 25% Nylon): 1 mini skein Orange Speckle (Yarn F)
Size US6 (4mm) 24" (60cm) circular needles or size needed to obtain gauge
Stitch marker
Tapestry needle

Gauge: 16 sts and 32 rows = 4 in/10cm.

CO 9 sts, using Yarn A.
Row 1 (RS): K1, yo, *k1, sl1pw (yarn at back), yo, pass k st over sl1 and yo; rep from * to marker, yo, PM, k3, PM, yo, *k1, sl1pw (yarn at back), yo, pass k st over sl1 and yo; rep from * to last st, yo, k1.
Row 2 (WS) and all even-numbered rows: Purl.
Row 3: K1, yo, *k1, sl1pw (yarn at back), yo, pass k st over sl1 and yo; rep from * to marker, yo, SM, k3, SM, yo, *k1, sl1pw (yarn at back), yo, pass k st over sl1 and yo; rep from * to last st, yo, k1.
Row 5: K1, yo, *k1, sl1pw (yarn at back), yo, pass k st over sl1 and yo; rep from * to marker, yo, SM, sl1, k2, psso the two sts, SM, yo, *k1, sl1pw (yarn at back), yo, pass k st over sl1 and yo; rep from * to last st, yo, k1.
Row 7: K1, yo, *k1, sl1pw (yarn at back), yo, pass k st over sl1 and yo; rep from * to marker, yo, SM, k1, yo, k1, SM, yo, *k1, sl1pw (yarn at back), yo, pass k st over sl1 and yo; rep from * to last st, yo, k1.

Altair Cowl

Inspired by Altair, the brightest star in the constellation of Aquila and the twelfth-brightest star in the night sky. Altair rotates rapidly, with the velocity at its equator resulting in a non-spherical shape. That shape is emulated in this seamless cowl design. It looks more complex than it is, making this a great project for anyone who can knit and purl in the round. In designing this, I focused on texture that could handle speckled or busy colorways.

Weight of Yarn: 3 Light
Skill Level: Intermediate

Sizes: One

Finished Measurements: Height: 21cm. Width: 28cm. Circumference: 56cm

Materials:
My Mama Knits PATSY DK (273yds/250m, 3.53oz/100g, 100% Superwash Merino Wool): 1 skein Ghost of Captain Cutler
Size US6 (4mm) 24" (60cm) circular needles or size needed to obtain gauge
Stitch marker
Tapestry needle

Gauge: In pattern stitch, 22 sts and 33 rounds = 4 in/10cm.

CO 127 sts. Knit first and last stitches together to join in the round, being careful not to twist. Mark start of round with stitch marker. (126 sts)

Edge Rounds 1-6: *P3, k3, rep from * to end of round.

Rounds 1-4: Knit.
Rounds 5-11: *K9, p5, k4; rep from * to end of round.
Rounds 12-17: Knit.
Rounds 18-24: *P5, k13; rep from * to end of round.
Rounds 25-26: Knit.
Repeat these 26 rounds until the piece measures 8-10" in height, or your desired size.

Edge Rounds 1-2: Knit.
Edge Rounds 3-8: *P3, k3, rep from * to end of round.

Bind off loosely. Block and weave in ends.

Betelgeuse Shawl

This single-skein bottom-up triangle shawl is knit flat. The nature of the construction also means it is flexible regarding yarn quantity and sizing - just use more yarn for a larger shawl. Named for one of the largest stars visible to the naked eye, Betelgeuse is the ninth-brightest star in the night sky and second-brightest in the constellation of Orion. The star itself is a distinct orange-red, much like this yarn when viewed under black light.

Weight of Yarn: 1 Super Fine
Skill Level: Intermediate

Finished Measurements: Height: 70cm. Width: 129cm

Materials:
Qing Fibre SINGLES (400yds/366m, 3.53oz/100g, 100% Superwash Merino Wool): 1 skein Firaja
Size US6 (4mm) 24" (60cm) circular needles or size needed to obtain gauge
Stitch marker
Tapestry needle

Gauge: In pattern stitch between eyelets, 20 sts and 32 rows = 4 in/10cm.

CO 3 sts.
Set up Row: Purl.
Row 1 (RS): K1, yo, knit to last st, yo, k1.
Row 2 (WS): K1, purl to last st, k1.
Repeat these two rows for the duration of the pattern, except for...

Rows 39-54, 63-78, 87-102, 111-126, 135-150, 159-174, 183-198, 207-222, 231-246, 255-270, 279-294, 303-318, 327-342, 351-366, 375-390, and 399-419. Work these rows as follows:

Rows 39, 43, 63, 67, 87, 91, 111, 115, 135, 139, 159, 163, 183, 187, 207, 211, 231, 235, 255, 259, 279, 283, 303, 307, 327, 331, 351, 355, 375, 379, 399, 403, 423, 427, 447, and 451 (RS):
K1, yo, k1, (k2, k2tog, yo, k8) three, five, or seven times as required; knit to last st, yo, k1.

Even-numbered rows 40-54, 64-78, and 88-102 (WS):
K1, purl to last st, k1.

Rows 41, 65, 89, 113, 137, 161, 185, 209, 233, 257, 281, 305, 329, 353, 377, 401, 425, and 449 (RS):
K1, yo, k1, (k1, k2tog, yo, k2tog, yo, k7) three, five, seven times as required; knit to last st, yo, k1.

Rows 45, 53, 69, 77, 93, 101, 117, 125, 141, 149, 165, 173, 189, 197, 213, 221, 237, 245, 261, 269, 285, 293, 309, 317, 333, 341, 357, 365, 381, 389, 405, 413, 429, 437, 453, and 461 (RS):
K1, yo, knit to last st, yo, k1.

Rows 47, 51, 71, 75, 95, 99, 119, 123, 143, 147, 167, 171, 191, 195, 215, 219, 239, 243, 263, 267, 287,

291, 311, 315, 335, 339, 359, 363, 383, 387, 407, 411, 431, 435, 455, and 459 (RS):
K1, yo, k1, (k8, k2tog, yo, k2) three, five, seven times as required; knit to last st, yo, k1.

Row 49, 73, 97, 121, 145, 169, 193, 217, 241, 265, 289, 313, 337, 361, 385, 409, 433, and 457 (RS):
K1, yo, k1, (k7, k2tog, yo, k2tog, yo, k1) three, five, seven times as required; knit to last st, yo, k1.

Stop when you are running short of yarn and then finish with nine rows in stockinette stitch, followed by six rows in garter stitch.

Bind off loosely using a stretchy bind-off technique. Block in a triangle shape. Weave in ends.

Cassiopeia Mini Skein Shawl

This pattern helps all the beautiful mini skeins you've collected shine. This shawl is knit on the bias with easy-to-memorize stitches, making for an approachable wrap. Knit it with eight skeins for Hanukkah, 24 for the Advent season, seven for a one-week shawl challenge - or just use this pattern with leftover scraps of various amounts for a fun, vibrant wrap. The stitch pattern emulates the constellation after which the pattern is named with subtle W-shaped eyelets.

Weight of Yarn: 1 Super Fine
Skill Level: Intermediate

Finished Measurements: Length: 50cm. Width: 242cm

Materials:
Eve Chambers Textiles SOCK MINI SKEINS (87yds/80m, 20g, 100% Superwash BFL): 2 skeins Sad Summer (Grey)
Mad Scientist Yarns SOCK STELLAR MINI SKEINS (87yds/80m, 20g, 75% Superwash Merino, 20% Nylon, 5% Silver Lurex): 1 skein Bonkers Biologist (Blue-Green)
Mad Scientist Yarns SOCK STELLAR MINI SKEINS (87yds/80m, 20g, 75% Superwash Merino, 20% Nylon, 5% Silver Lurex): 1 skein Phunky Physicist (Purple)
Mad Scientist Yarns SOCK STELLAR MINI SKEINS (87yds/80m, 20g, 75% Superwash Merino, 20% Nylon, 5% Silver Lurex): 1 skein Crazy Chemist (Grey-Green)
Mad Scientist Yarns SOCK STELLAR MINI SKEINS (87yds/80m, 20g, 75% Superwash Merino, 20% Nylon, 5% Silver Lurex): 1 skein Mad Scientist (Citrus Yellow)
Mad Scientist Yarns SOCK STELLAR MINI SKEINS (87yds/80m, 20g, 75% Superwash Merino, 20% Nylon, 5% Silver Lurex): 1 skein Erratic Engineer (Orange-Peach)
Mad Scientist Yarns SOCK STELLAR MINI SKEINS (87yds/80m, 20g, 75% Superwash Merino, 20% Nylon, 5% Silver Lurex): 1 skein Apoplectic Engineer (Bright Green)
Mothy and the Squid 4-PLY SOCK MINI SKEINS (91yds/84m, 20g, 75% Merino Wool, 25% Nylon): 1 skein Waterlilies (Aqua-Pink)
Mothy and the Squid 4-PLY SOCK MINI SKEINS (91yds/84m, 20g, 75% Merino Wool, 25% Nylon): 1 skein Blue Raspberry (Blue-Pink)
Mothy and the Squid 4-PLY SOCK MINI SKEINS (91yds/84m, 20g, 75% Merino Wool, 25% Nylon): 1 skein Japanese Maple Leaves (Brown-Pink)
My Mama Knits CHOUFUNGA SOCK MINI SKEINS (92yds/85m, 20g, 75% Merino, 25% Nylon): 1 skein Stardust (Purple)
My Mama Knits CHOUFUNGA SOCK MINI SKEINS (92yds/85m, 20g, 75% Merino, 25% Nylon): 1 skein You Shoot Like Girls (Pink-Green)
My Mama Knits CHOUFUNGA SOCK MINI SKEINS (92yds/85m, 20g, 75% Merino, 25% Nylon): 1 skein That's a Manly Name (Grey-Green)
My Mama Knits CHOUFUNGA SOCK MINI SKEINS (92yds/85m, 20g, 75% Merino, 25% Nylon): 1 skein Bee Mine (Grey-Pink-Yellow)
My Mama Knits CHOUFUNGA SOCK MINI SKEINS (92yds/85m, 20g, 75% Merino, 25% Nylon): 1 skein Pumpkin Patch Party (Orange)
Size US6 (4mm) 24" (60cm) circular needles or size needed to obtain gauge
Stitch marker
Tapestry needle

Gauge: In pattern stitch 30 sts and 32 rows = 4 in/10cm.

CO 138 sts with a stretchy or long-tail cast on.
Row 1 (RS): Sl1kw, k2, kfb, *k1, yo, k3, sl1kw, k2tog, psso, k3, yo; rep from * until 4 sts remain, k2tog, k2.
Row 2 (WS) and all even-numbered rows: Sl1kw, k2, purl until 3 sts remain, k3.
Row 3: Sl1kw, k2, kfb, *k2, yo, k2, sl1kw, k2tog, psso, k2, yo, k1; rep from * until 4 sts remain, k2tog, k2.
Row 5: Sl1kw, k2, kfb, *k3, yo, k1, sl1kw, k2tog, psso, k1, yo, k2; rep from * until 4 sts remain, k2tog, k2.
Row 7: Sl1kw, k2, kfb, *k4, yo, sl1kw, k2tog, psso, yo, k3; rep from * until 4 sts remain, k2tog, k2.

Repeat until yarn runs out, switching mini-skeins as you go. This can be done mid-row if you like.

Bind off loosely.
Block and weave in ends.

Elara Shawl

Elara is the eighth-largest moon of Jupiter. This design reflects the moon's shape through purl stitches, eyelets, and bobbles. This shawl has a triangle shape, but feels elegant with the alternating textures and bobbles. This is a nice size for warmth while eyelets still showing off the outfit beneath, making this a choice project for a special event or to go with a favorite occasion dress.

Weight of Yarn: 1 Super Fine
Skill Level: Intermediate

Finished Measurements: Height: 69cm. Width: 150cm

Materials:
Eve Chambers Textiles SOCK (437yds/400m, 100g, 75% Superwash Merino Wool, 25% Silk): 2 skeins Flamingo Moon
Size US6 (4mm) 24" (60cm) circular needles or size needed to obtain gauge
Stitch marker
Tapestry needle

Gauge: In purl pattern stitch, 18 sts and 40 rounds = 4 in/10cm.

CO 17 sts, placing markers on both sides of center st.

Purl Set:
Row 1 (RS): K1, yo, knit to last st before marker, kfb, SM, k1, SM, kfb, knit to last st, yo, k1.
Rows 2 and 4 (WS): K1, purl to last st, k1.
Row 3: K1, yo, *k3, p1; rep from * to last st before marker, kfb, SM, k1, SM, kfb, *p1, k3; rep from * to last st, yo, k1.
Repeat this set of 4 rows three more times; then work the Garter Stitch Set.
(49 sts) Stitch count per increase row: 21, 25, 29, 33, 37, 41, 45, 49

Garter Stitch Set:
Rows 9, 11, 13, and 15 (RS): K1, yo, knit until last st before marker, kfb, SM, k1, SM, kfb, knit to last st, yo, k1.
Rows 10, 12, and 14 (WS): Knit.
Row 16: K1, purl to last st, k1.
Work this set of rows once; then knit the alternating pattern set (if you just knit the Purl Set, proceed to the Eyelet Set, for example).
(65 sts) Stitch count per increase row: 53, 57, 61, 65

Eyelet Set:
Row 1 (RS): K1, yo, knit to last st before marker, kfb, SM, k1, SM, kfb, knit to last st, yo, k1.
Rows 2 and 4 (WS): K1, purl to last st, k1.
Row 3: K1, yo, *k2, k2tog, yo; rep from * to last st before marker, kfb, SM, k1, SM, kfb, *yo, ssk, k2; rep from * to last st, yo, k1.

Repeat this set of 4 rows three more times; then work the Garter Stitch Set..
(97 sts) Stitch count per increase row: 69, 73, 77, 81 85, 89 93, 97

Repeat the three pattern sets in that order one more time before proceeding to the Bobble Set.

Bobble Set:

Technical note:
Bobble is made as follows: Kfb into the same stitch 3 times, then pass the last 5 sts over the first one.

Row 1 (RS): K1, *p3, make bobble, k2; rep from * to last st before marker, k1, SM, k1, SM, k1, *k2, make bobble, p3; rep from * to last st, k1.
Row 2 (WS): K1, *k3, p3; rep from * to last st before marker, p1, SM, p1, SM, p1, *p3, k3; rep from * to last st, k1.
Row 3: K1, *p2, make bobble, k2, p1; rep from * to last st before marker, k1, SM, k1, SM, k1, *p1, k2, make bobble, p2; rep from * to last st, k1.
Row 4: K1, *p2, k3, p1; rep from * to last st before marker, p1, SM, p1, SM, p1, *p1, k3, p2; rep from * to last st, k1.
Row 5: K1, *p1, make bobble, k2, p2; rep from * to last st before marker, k1, SM, k1, SM, k1, *p2, k2, make bobble, p1; rep from * to last st, k1.
Row 6: K1, *p1, k3, p2; rep from * to last st before marker, p1, SM, p1, SM, p1, *p2, k3, p1; rep from * to last st, k1.
Row 7: K4, *p3, make bobble, k2; rep from * to 4 sts before marker, p3, k1, SM, k1, SM, k1, p3, *k2, make bobble, p3; rep from * to last 4 sts, k4.
Row 8: K1, p3, *k3, p3; rep from * to 5 sts before marker, k3, p2, SM, p1, SM, p2, *k3, p3; rep from * to last 7 sts, k3, p3, k1.
Row 9: K1, *k2, p3, make bobble, k1; rep from * to last st before marker, k1, SM, k1, SM, k1, *k1, make bobble, p3, k2; rep from * to last st, k1.
Row 10: K1, p1, *k3, p3; rep from * to 5 sts before marker, k3, p2, SM, p1, SM, p2, *k3, p3; rep from * to last 5 sts, k3, p1, k1.

Picot bind-off (right side of your work): Cast on 2 sts; bind off 4 stitches. Move remaining loop on right-hand needle to left-hand needle. Continue sequence across row until all sts are bound off.
Block and weave in ends.

Sample shown features six pattern repeats, bordered by garter sections, with the bobble section at the end.

Firefly Hour Mitts

Our hands have to deal with all the elements and with work, from washing dishes to weeding the garden, but they take on an almost magical softness when we cup them to briefly hold a caught firefly. When I saw La Bien Aimee's Pop Grunge colorway, it reminded me of those childhood moments of running around the garden at twilight amidst the twinkle of emerging fireflies. The ruffled edge winds like the paths of the insects. The ribbed nature of the knitting and the lack of thumb gusset in this pattern, making make it a quick knit that works for a range of hand sizes.

Weight of Yarn: 3 Light
Skill Level: Intermediate

Sizes: One

Finished Measurements: Length: 27cm. Width: 6.5cm. Circumference: 14cm

Materials:
Pink Ruffle version:
La Bien Aimee MERINO DK (252yds/230m, 4.06oz/115g, 100% Superwash Merino): 1 skein Pop Grunge (Grey) (Yarn A) - 73g used for one pair of mitts
Uschitita 4-PLY SINGLES (400yds/366m, 3/5oz/100g, 100% Superwash Merino): 1 skein Strangelove (Pink) (Yarn B) - 17g used for ruffles for two pair of mitts and a small swatch
Yellow Ruffle version:
GamerCrafting DK SOCK (246yds/225m, 100g, 75% Superwash Merino Wool, 25% Nylon): 1 skein Reverse Rave-Icorn (Rainbow) (Yarn A) - 64g used for one pair of mitts
GamerCrafting 4-PLY (437yds/400m, 100g, 100% Superwash Merino Wool): 1 skein High Voltage (Yellow) (Yarn B) - 7g used for ruffles for two pair of mitts and a small swatch
Size US7 (4.5mm) 24" (60cm) circular needles or size needed to obtain gauge
Size US6 (4mm) 24" (60cm) circular needles or size needed to obtain gauge
Stitch marker
Tapestry needle

Gauge: In Stockinette stitch on US7 (4.5mm) needles, 11.5 sts and 14.5 rnds = 4 in/10cm.
In pattern stitch on US7 (4.5mm) needles, 16 sts and 27 rows = 4 in/10cm.

CO 40 sts, using Yarn A and larger needles. Join in the round, being careful not to twist. Mark start of round with stitch marker.

Rounds 1-7: *K1, p1; rep from * to end of round.

Round 8: *K1, p1; rep from * until 2 sts remain, then BO and continue to the next round.

Rows 9-15 (these rows are knit flat): *K1, p1; rep from * to end of row.

Row 16 (RS): *K1, p1; rep from * until 2 sts remain, then kfb twice, and then rejoin in the round.

Rounds 17-61: *K1, p1; rep from * to end of round.

Change to Yarn B and smaller needles:

Rounds 62-66 & 68 & 70: Knit.

Rounds 67 & 69: *Kfb; rep from * to end of round.

Round 71: Purl.

Bind off.
Weave in ends.

Midnight Waffles Cowl

The Midnight Waffles pattern looks complex, but is a simple combination of slipped, knit, and purl stitches. The cowl design features a provisional cast on that is later joined with the bind-off edge for a continuous pattern and double the insulation. The resulting cowl works equally well as a headband/earwarmer. The name is inspired by my mother's tradition of taking me out to the all-night diner for waffles when she finished a wallpaper or DIY project on our home. It was one of the early ways she included me in home improvement projects even before I could wield a putty knife or hammer. It was made all the more special that the diner had a sister location which is where my parents went on their first date. Midnight Waffles celebrates the little wins that make big memories.

Weight of Yarn: 3 Light
Skill Level: Intermediate

Sizes: One

Finished Measurements:
Height: 23.5cm tall before seaming; 11.5cm after seaming.
Width: 24cm. Circumference: 47.5cm after seaming

Materials:
My Mama Knits PATSY DK (273yds/250m, 3.53oz/100g, 100% Superwash Merino): 1 skein each Hen Party (Yarn A) and Sugar Skull (Yarn B)
Size US6 (4mm) 24" (60cm) circular needles or size needed to obtain gauge
Stitch marker
Waste yarn
Tapestry needle

Gauge: In stockinette stitch, 22 sts and 15 rnds = 4 in/10cm. In pattern, 32 rows and 24 sts = 4 in/10cm.

CO 125 sts, using yarn A and a stretchy provisional cast-on (you will be joining the final edge to the cast-on edge at the end of the project). Slip the first stitch to be next to the last on the needle then knit those two together to join in the round. Place a stitch marker to indicate the beginning of the round. (124 sts)

Round 1 (Yarn A): *K1, p3; rep from * to end of round.
Rounds 2-4 (Yarn B): *Sl 1 kw wyib, k3, rep from * to end of round.
Round 5 (Yarn A): Knit.

Repeat rounds 1-5 a total of 20-30 times.
Join final edge to the provisional cast-on edge using the Kitchener Stitch.

Block and weave in ends.

Phare Hat

Inspired by lighthouses perched on the coastline, I named this hat pattern for the French word for lighthouse. With slipped stitches and textures to emulate the beacon of light. The hat pattern has three sizes and can be topped off with a pompom.

Weight of Yarn: 4 Medium
Skill Level: Intermediate

Sizes: Small (Medium, Large) = 37 (44, 50) cm circumference

Finished Measurements:
Small: Circumference: 38cm. Height: 21cm (without pom pom)
Medium: Circumference: 44cm. Height: 21.5cm (without pom pom)
Large: Circumference: 50.5cm. Height: 22cm (without pom pom)

Materials:
Bear In Sheep's Clothing HAND-DYED BEAR COSY ARAN (174yds/160m, 100g, 100% Falkland Merino Wool): 1 skein Concrete Jungle-Speckle Gradient
Size US8 (5mm) and US10 (6mm) 24" (60cm) circular needles or size needed to obtain gauge
US10 (6mm) double-pointed needles (optional)
Stitch marker
Tapestry needle

Gauge: In pattern, 24 sts and 32 rows = 4 in/10cm

CO 72 (84, 96) sts with the smaller needles, using a tubular or long-tail cast-on. Join in the round, being careful not to twist. Place a stitch marker to indicate the beginning of the round.
Set-up Rounds (6 rounds using the smaller needles): *K4, p2; rep from * to end of round.

Switch to larger needles.
Rounds 1-6: *K4, p2; rep from * to end of round.
Round 7: *Insert the right needle after the fourth stitch and create a loop by wrapping the yarn around the needle, pulling it back through, and placing this new stitch on the left needle, next to the first stitch. Knit the new loop stitch and the first stitch together through the back, k3, p2; rep from * to end of round.
Rounds 8, 10, 12, 14, and 16: *K4, p2; rep from * to end of round.
Rounds 9, 11, and 13: K1, p2, *k4, p2; rep from * to last st, k1.
Round 15: K1, p2, *create a loop as in Round 7, k3, p2; rep from * to last st, k1.
Repeat rounds 1-16 until the hat measures 5.5cm from edge (you may end mid-repeat if you wish, as long as you end after a Round 1–6, 8, 10, 12, 14, 15, or 16).

Decrease Rounds (use the Magic Loop method or DPNs for this section):
Round 1: *K4, p2; rep from * to end of round.
Round 2: *K2, k2tog, p2; rep from * to end of round. (60 (72, 84) sts)

Round 3: *K3, p2; rep from * to end of round.
Round 4: *K3, p2tog; rep from * to end of round. (48 (60, 72) sts)
Round 5: *K3, p1; rep from * to end of round.
Round 6: *K1, k2tog, p1; rep from * to end of round. (36 (48, 60) sts)
Round 7: *K2, p1; rep from * to end of round.
Round 8: *K2tog, p1; rep from * to end of round. (24 (36, 48) sts)
Round 9: *K1, p1; rep from * to end of round.
Round 10: *K2tog; rep from * to end of round. (12 (24, 36) sts)

Repeat Round 10 once for size Small, twice for size Medium, and three times for size Large; then break the yarn and weave in ends.

Porch Light Wrap

The warm illumination of a porch light shares its beam to cast shadows and play with light in the night. Insects flock to its mesmerizing glow. This fun, sideways asymmetrical triangle shawl grows as you knit it. You can keep going as long as you like - or your skeins allow - making this a flexible pattern.

Weight of Yarn: 1 Super Fine
Skill Level: Intermediate

Finished Measurements: Length: 170cm. Width: 4cm (at the starting end) and 133cm (at the widest end)

Materials:
Martin's Lab BOUNCY SPORT (328yds/300m, 100g, 100% High Twist Superwash Merino): 1 skein Highlite (Yarn A)
My Mama Knits CHOUFUNGA SOCK (465yds/425m, 100g, 75% Merino Wool, 25% Nylon): 1 skein Girly Girl (Yarn B)
Green Elephant Yarn BFL SOCK (437yds/400m, 100g, 100% SW Bluefaced Leicester): 1 skein Rosa (Yarn C)
Size US6 (4mm) 24" (60cm) circular needles or size needed to obtain gauge
Stitch marker
Tapestry needle

Gauge: In stockinette stitch, 23 sts and 33 rows = 4 in/10cm.

Switch between Yarn A and Yarn B every four rows until Yarn A runs out; then switch between Yarn B and Yarn C until Yarn B runs out; and then complete pattern with Yarn C only.

CO 4 sts using Yarn A.
Set-up Rows 1, 3, and 5: Kfb, knit to the last stitch, kfb.
Set up Rows 2, 4 and 6: K2, purl to the last 2 sts, k2. (10 sts)

Row 1 (RS): K2, *yo, k2tog, k4, rep from * to last 2 sts, kfb, k1.
All Even-Numbered Rows (WS): K2, purl to the last 2 sts, k2.
Row 3: K2, *k1, yo, k2tog, k3; rep from * to last 2 sts, kfb, k1.
Row 5: K2, *k2, yo, k2tog, k2; rep from * to last 2 sts, kfb, k1.
Row 7: K2, *k3, yo, k2tog, k1; rep from * to last 2 sts, kfb, k1.
Row 9: K2, *k4, yo, k2tog; rep from * to last 2 sts, kfb, k1.
Row 11: K2, *k3, yo, k2tog, k1; rep from * to last 2 sts, kfb, k1.
Row 13: K2, *k2, yo, k2tog, k2; rep from * to last 2 sts, kfb, k1.
Row 15: K2, *k1, yo, k2tog, k3; rep from * to last 2 sts, kfb, k1.

Repeat these 15 rows to form pattern, switching colors as instructed above. Knit until all the yarn is used.
Bind off loosely. Block gently into shape. Weave in ends.

Rigel Cowl

Rigel is the brightest star in the constellation of Orion. The star looks blue-white to the naked eye. Knit from the top down, this cowl is soft and a fun way to use special buttons. The stitch pattern is my Colorway Accented Stockinette. Similar to the approach used for the Rigel Mitts, this pattern spotlights small bursts of color, making it ideal for colorways with a dominant color accented by a mini rainbow or speckles.

Weight of Yarn: 4 Medium
Skill Level: Intermediate

Finished Measurements: Length: 18.5cm. Width: 26.5cm. Circumference: 52cm

Materials:
Fibre Art Studio Superwash Merino Worsted (240yds/219m, 110g, 100% wool): 1 skein And The Winner Is...
Size US9 (5.5mm) 24" (60cm) circular needles or size needed to obtain gauge
Stitch marker
Tapestry needle
Three buttons

Gauge: In pattern stitch, 20 sts and 27 rounds = 4in/10cm.

Colorway Accented Stockinette Pattern:
In the round:
Knit (each time you encounter a non-dominant color on the needle, purl it instead).
Flat:
Odd rows: Knit (each time you encounter a non-dominant color on the needle, purl it instead).
Even rows: Purl (each time you encounter a non-dominant color on the needle, knit it instead).

CO 102 sts.
Top Ribbing and Button Band:
Rows 1, 3, and 5 (RS): K9, *p3, k1; rep from * to last 9 sts, k9.
Rows 2 and 4 (WS): K9, *p1, k3; rep from * to last 9 sts, k9.
Row 6: K4, yo, k1, k2tog, k2, Colorway Accented Stockinette Pattern worked flat to last 9 sts, k9.
Rows 7, 9, 11, 13, 15, 17, 19, 21, 23, 25, and 27: K9, Colorway Accented Stockinette Pattern worked flat to last 9 sts, k9.
Rows 8, 10, 14, 16, 20, 22, and 26: K9, Colorway Accented Stockinette Pattern worked flat to last 9 sts, k9.
Rows 12, 18, and 24: K4, yo, k1, k2tog, k2, Colorway Accented Stockinette Pattern worked flat to last 9 sts, k9.
Row 28: Bind off 9 sts, Colorway Accented Stockinette Pattern worked flat to last 9 sts, k9.
Row 29: K9, Colorway Accented Stockinette Pattern worked flat. Join in the round (bypassing bound off stitches which you'll later seam).

Body of Cowl:
All Rounds: Colorway Accented Stockinette Pattern worked in the round.

Bottom Ribbing:
Rounds 1-6: K9, *p3, k1; rep from * to last 9 sts, k9.

Bind off loosely. Seam the back of the button band at the base to the main cowl section using the same yarn.

Block. Sew on buttons. Weave in ends.

Rigel Mitts

Similar to the approach in the Rigel Cowl, this pattern spotlights small bursts of color, making it ideal for colorways with a dominant color accented by a mini rainbow or speckles.

Weight of Yarn: 1 Super Fine
Skill Level: Intermediate

Finished Measurements: Length: 15cm. Width: 8.5cm. Circumference: 18cm

Materials:
The Wool Kitchen BFL DK (246yds/225m, 100g, 100% Superwash BFL): 1 skein Cosmic Girl Dark
Size US6 (4mm) 24" (60cm) circular needles or size needed to obtain gauge
Stitch marker
Tapestry needle

Gauge: In stockinette stitch, 20 sts and 28 rounds = 4in/10cm.

Colorway Accented Ribbing Pattern:
In the round:
*K3, p1; rep from * to end of round (each time you encounter a non-dominant color on the needle, purl it instead).
Flat:
Odd rows: *K3, p1; rep from * to end of row (each time you encounter a non-dominant color on the needle, purl it instead).
Even rows: *k1, P3; rep from * to end of row (each time you encounter a non-dominant color on the needle, knit it instead).

CO 40 sts. Join in the round, being careful not to twist. Mark start of round with a stitch marker.
Rounds 1-20: Colorway Accented Ribbing worked in the round.
Round 21: *K3, p1; rep from * to end of round.
Reverse direction and work the next rows flat, beginning with Row 22, a WS row.
Rows 22-28: Colorway Accented Ribbing worked flat.
Round 29: Rejoin sts. Colorway Accented Ribbing worked in the round.
Rounds 30-49: Colorway Accented Ribbing worked in the round.
Bind off loosely. Weave in ends.

Wreath Nebula Mitts

There is something so satisfying about quick knits that are also soft and cosy. Using two colors of DK yarn, these mitts are knit flat, top down, and seamed up the side, leaving an opening for the thumb. Just weave in the ends and start keeping your hands warm! Like the other two mitt patterns in this collection, the result fits either the right and left hand - which means if you have enough yarn you can make a third as a spare in case one gets lost.

Weight of Yarn: 3 Light
Skill Level: Intermediate

Sizes: One

Finished Measurements: Length: 14.5cm. Center Width: 9cm. Circumference: 18cm

Materials:
Green Elephant DK (273yds/250m, 100g, 100% Superwash Merino Wool): 1 skein Zest (Yarn A)
Green Elephant DK (273yds/250m, 100g, 100% Superwash Merino Wool): 1 skein Bellyflop (Yarn B)
Size US6 (4mm) needles or size needed to obtain gauge for ribbing
Size US8 (5mm) needles or size needed to obtain gauge for pattern stitch
Tapestry needle

Gauge: In main pattern stitch, 22sts and 44rows = 4 in/10cm.

CO 40 sts with Yarn A using 4mm needles.
Rows 1-12: *K2, P2; rep from * to end of row.
Switch to 5mm knitting needles and use Yarn B.
RS Odd Rows: K1 *sl1 pw wyif, K1; rep from * to last st, k1.
WS Even Rows: P1 *sl1 pw wyib, P1; rep from * to last st, p1.
Switch to 4mm knitting needles and use Yarn A.
Rows 42-48: *K2, P2; rep from * to end of row.

Bind off. Block. Seam up sides, leaving an opening for each thumbhole. Weave in ends.

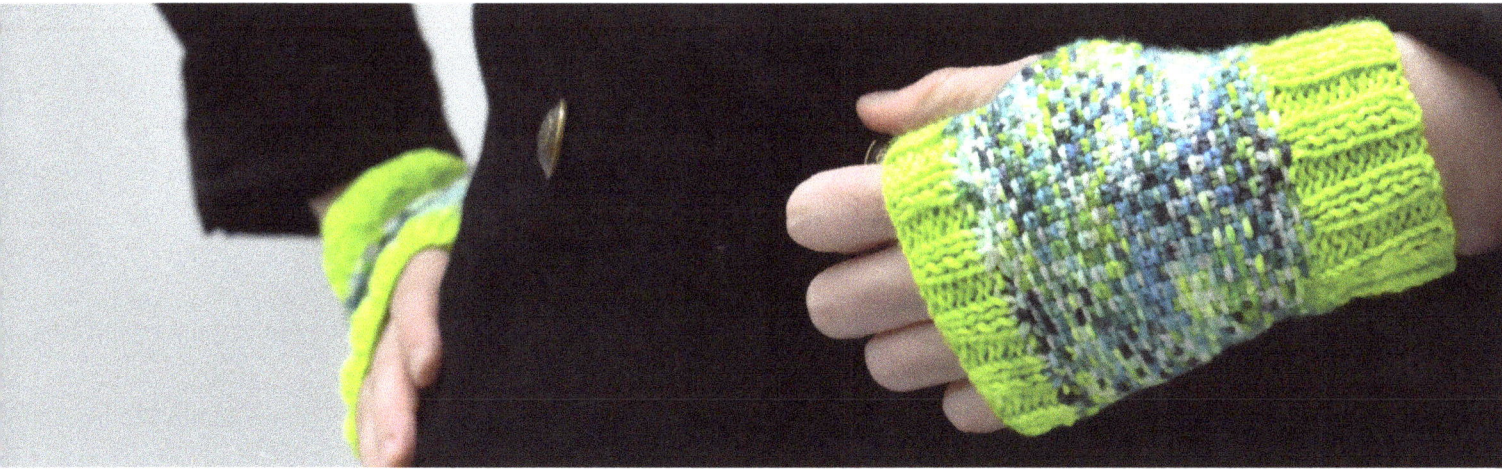

www.ingramcontent.com/pod-product-compliance
Lightning Source LLC
Chambersburg PA
CBHW042017090526
44588CB00024B/2893